What Are They Made Of?

Julie Haydon

Contents

The Gate	2
The Digger	4
The Swing	6
The Hammock	8
The Slide	10
The Tower	12
The Net	14
Glossary	16

The Gate

Dad and I go to the park.

We go in the gate.

The gate is made of metal.

The Digger

I sit on the digger.
The bucket goes
up and down.

The digger is made of metal, too.

The Swing

I play on the swing.

I go up and down.

The swing is made of rubber.

The Hammock

I play on the **hammock**.

Dad swings it for me.

The hammock is made of rubber, too.

The Slide

I go into the big slide.

I come down the slide.

The slide is made of plastic.

The Tower

Dad and I go up the tower.

The tower is made of wood.

The Net

I play on the big net. My hands and feet are on the net.

The net is made of **rope**.

Glossary

hammock

rope